GOLF JOKES

TO ROAST YOUR BUDDY

155 HILARIOUS
YOUR GOLF GAME IS SO BAD...
JOKES

BY
OSSY SCOTT
Budir Publishing

©Copyright 2024 Ossy Scott
All rights reserved.
ISBN: 9798344784687
No part of this book may be reproduced or used in any manner without the prior written permission of the copyright owner, except for the use of brief quotations in a book review.

For every golfer who's made a divot
bigger than their last paycheck.
Keep swinging!

Don't miss the bonus section at the end!

THE ULTIMATE LIST OF CHEERS FOR THE 19TH HOLE

Introduction

Welcome to ***Golf Jokes to Roast Your Buddy***, the ultimate collection of one liner jabs and roasts made for every golfer who loves the game—and knows how to laugh at the many misfires that come with it.

Whether you're a weekend warrior, a seasoned fairway prowler, or a reluctant caddie to your best friend's shanked shots, this book is here to give you and your buddies something to chuckle about as you navigate the highs and lows of the course.

Inside these pages, you'll find 155 of the finest roasts tailored to hit all the classic golf mishaps. From "frequent flyer miles" in the water hazards to drives that barely make it past the tee box, these jokes are designed to poke fun at the game we love while making it clear: sometimes, it's all about the laugh, not the score.

Plus, I've included a bonus section at the end -- **The Ultimate List of Cheers for the 19th Hole** so you can keep the laughs rolling after the round is over.

So grab a drink, settle into the cart, and get ready to rib your golf buddies like never before. Here's to the hooks, slices, divots, and disasters that make golf both endlessly frustrating and endlessly fun.

-Ossy

Section 1
155 Hilarious
one-line jokes that start with

Your golf game is so bad...

YOUR GOLF GAME IS SO BAD...

Your golf game is so bad that you've spent more time in the woods than a park ranger.

Your golf game is so bad that you've hit every water hazard except the drinking fountain.

Your golf game is so bad that your clubs are considering filing for divorce.

Your golf game is so bad that you need a lifeguard, not a caddie.

YOUR GOLF GAME IS SO BAD...

Your golf game is so bad that the trees are starting to duck when you tee off.

Your golf game is so bad that the sand traps have your name on speed dial.

Your golf game is so bad that even your caddie needs a drink after nine holes.

Your golf game is so bad that the bunkers have "Welcome" signs for you.

YOUR GOLF GAME IS SO BAD...

Your golf game is so bad that the water hazards started calling you by name.

Your golf game is so bad that the only thing you're under is pressure.

Your golf game is so bad that your driver applied for early retirement.

Your golf game is so bad that you get a hole-in-one... in the parking lot.

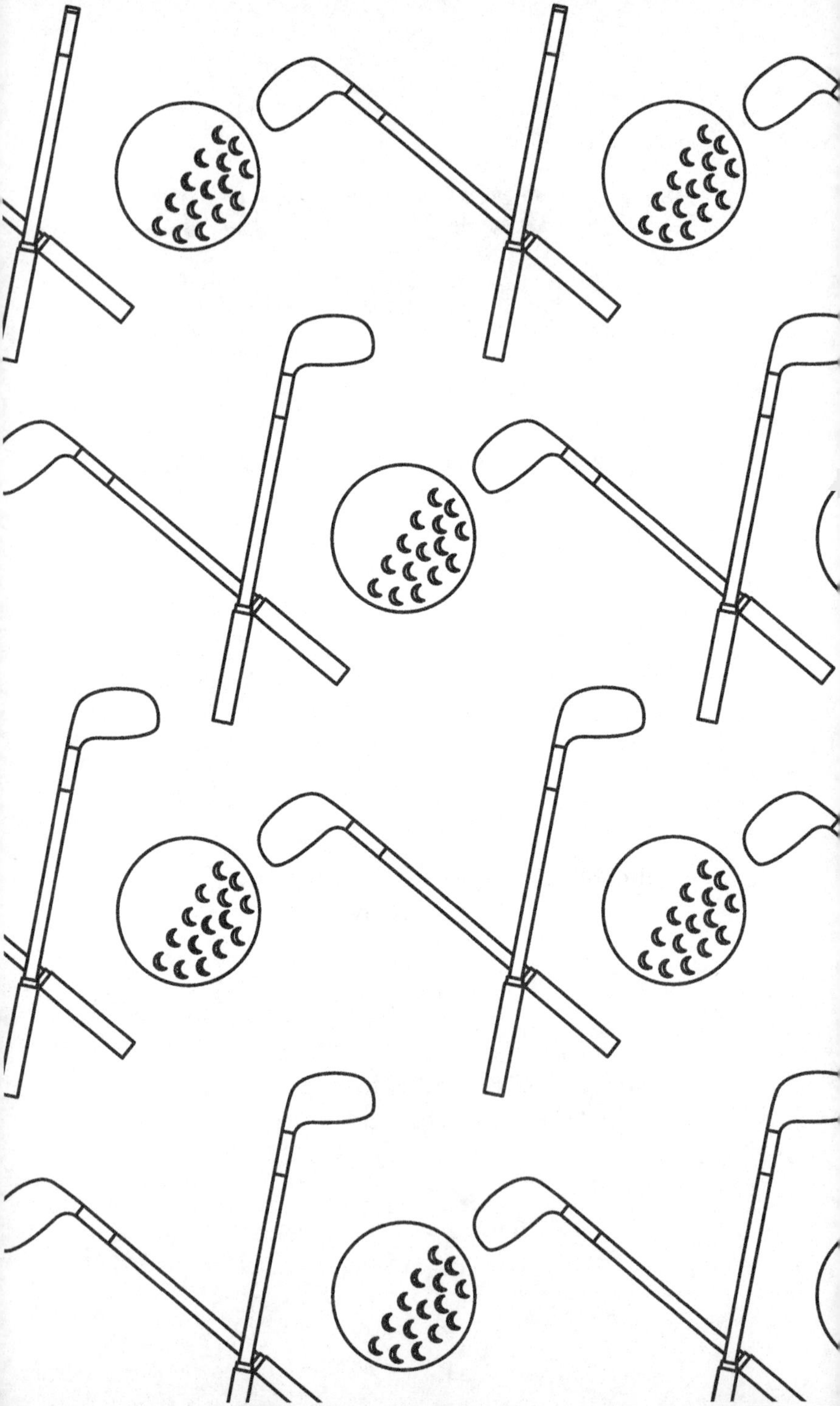

YOUR GOLF GAME IS SO BAD...

Your golf game is so bad that the golf ball leaves on vacation before you swing.

Your golf game is so bad that you bring more balls to the course than the pro shop has in stock.

Your golf game is so bad that even the ball washer gave up on you.

Your golf game is so bad that your bag has a permanent 'Lost and Found' section.

Your golf game is so bad that the course gives you frequent flyer miles.

YOUR GOLF GAME IS SO BAD...

Your golf game is so bad that even the squirrels laugh when you tee off.

Your golf game is so bad that you need Google Maps to find your ball.

Your golf game is so bad that your divots are larger than the green.

Your golf game is so bad that the greenskeeper asked you to stop aerating the course with your divots.

YOUR GOLF GAME IS SO BAD...

Your golf game is so bad that you could lose a ball in a sandbox.

Your golf game is so bad that you're on a first-name basis with every tree on the course.

Your golf game is so bad that your 9-iron is now a 3-wood —after you threw it against a tree.

Your golf game is so bad that the driving range banned you for endangering other players.

YOUR GOLF GAME IS SO BAD...

Your golf game is so bad that the only thing straight is your pencil stroke on the scorecard.

Your golf game is so bad that you've been asked to leave the putting green for taking too long.

Your golf game is so bad that even your glove threw in the towel.

Your golf game is so bad that you turn "Mulligan" into a lifestyle.

YOUR GOLF GAME IS SO BAD...

Your golf game is so bad that your score gets reported to Ripley's Believe It or Not.

Your golf game is so bad that the only thing you're consistently hitting is your ego.

Your golf game is so bad that the club pro asked if you were there for landscaping.

Your golf game is so bad that you make Happy Gilmore look like Tiger Woods.

YOUR GOLF GAME IS SO BAD...

Your golf game is so bad that your ball retriever gets more action than your driver.

Your golf game is so bad that the flagstick moves out of the way when you're putting.

Your golf game is so bad that the only "chip" you succeed at involves salsa.

Your golf game is so bad that you bring a metal detector instead of a club to find your ball.

YOUR GOLF GAME IS SO BAD...

Your golf game is so bad that the cart path is the only thing you can hit consistently.

Your golf game is so bad that your clubs came with a free gift—a resignation letter.

Your golf game is so bad that you're the reason they added extra balls to the range buckets.

Your golf game is so bad that the ball asked for a new owner.

YOUR GOLF GAME IS SO BAD...

Your golf game is so bad that your tee shots come with a soundtrack of crying birds.

Your golf game is so bad that even the wind changes direction to avoid helping you.

Your golf game is so bad that the GPS on the cart just says, "Good luck."

Your golf game is so bad that even the caddy is taking bets against you.

YOUR GOLF GAME IS SO BAD...

Your golf game is so bad that you've started naming the trees you keep hitting.

Your golf game is so bad that even your practice swings have gone missing.

Your golf game is so bad that you've got more lost balls than Tiger has wins.

Your golf game is so bad that you can't tell the difference between a golf bag and a survival kit.

YOUR GOLF GAME IS SO BAD...

Your golf game is so bad that your caddie needs hazard pay.

Your golf game is so bad that even the bunker started feeling sorry for you.

Your golf game is so bad that your driver filed for unemployment.

Your golf game is so bad that the fairway has become an urban legend in your round.

Your golf game is so bad that even your scorecard walks away in shame.

YOUR GOLF GAME IS SO BAD...

Your golf game is so bad that the wind adjusts to make sure you miss.

Your golf game is so bad that your golf shoes are the only thing seeing any action.

Your golf game is so bad that you've got a "frequent visitor" card for the rough.

Your golf game is so bad that even the scorecard asked to be excused.

YOUR GOLF GAME IS SO BAD...

Your golf game is so bad that you've got more excuses than clubs in your bag.

Your golf game is so bad that your swing's been classified as a natural disaster.

Your golf game is so bad that you've started asking the course marshal for search-and-rescue assistance.

Your golf game is so bad that the local wildlife avoids you for fear of getting hit.

YOUR GOLF GAME IS SO BAD...

Your golf game is so bad that the cart path has become your favorite fairway.

Your golf game is so bad that your clubs send postcards from the bottom of the lake.

Your golf game is so bad that even your rangefinder is out of ideas.

Your golf game is so bad that you could turn a 9-hole round into a day trip.

YOUR GOLF GAME IS SO BAD...

Your golf game is so bad that the only thing you've mastered is losing balls.

Your golf game is so bad that you have a permanent reservation in the sand traps.

Your golf game is so bad that you've started wearing a life vest to play near the water hazards.

Your golf game is so bad that the ball boy gave up retrieving your shots.

YOUR GOLF GAME IS SO BAD...

Your golf game is so bad that your scorecard looks like it's been attacked by a calculator.

Your golf game is so bad that even the cart GPS tells you to "recalculate."

Your golf game is so bad that the birds fly in formation to avoid your tee shots.

Your golf game is so bad that you've been asked to stop "redecorating" the course with your divots.

YOUR GOLF GAME IS SO BAD...

Your golf game is so bad that the geese on the course have declared a no-fly zone around you.

Your golf game is so bad that the course has started charging you for environmental damage.

Your golf game is so bad that your favorite club is the one that stays in the bag.

Your golf game is so bad that the ball fears for its life when it sees you approaching.

YOUR GOLF GAME IS SO BAD...

Your golf game is so bad that you need a chiropractor after every swing.

Your golf game is so bad that you've started bringing a fishing pole instead of a driver.

Your golf game is so bad that even the pros use your round as a "what not to do" example.

Your golf game is so bad that your buddies started charging admission just to watch.

YOUR GOLF GAME IS SO BAD...

Your golf game is so bad that the golf course is considering adding bumpers to the fairway—just for you.

Your golf game is so bad that you've lost more balls than a toy store.

Your golf game is so bad that the windmill on the mini-golf course told you to quit.

Your golf game is so bad that the local park service added your face to the wildlife caution signs.

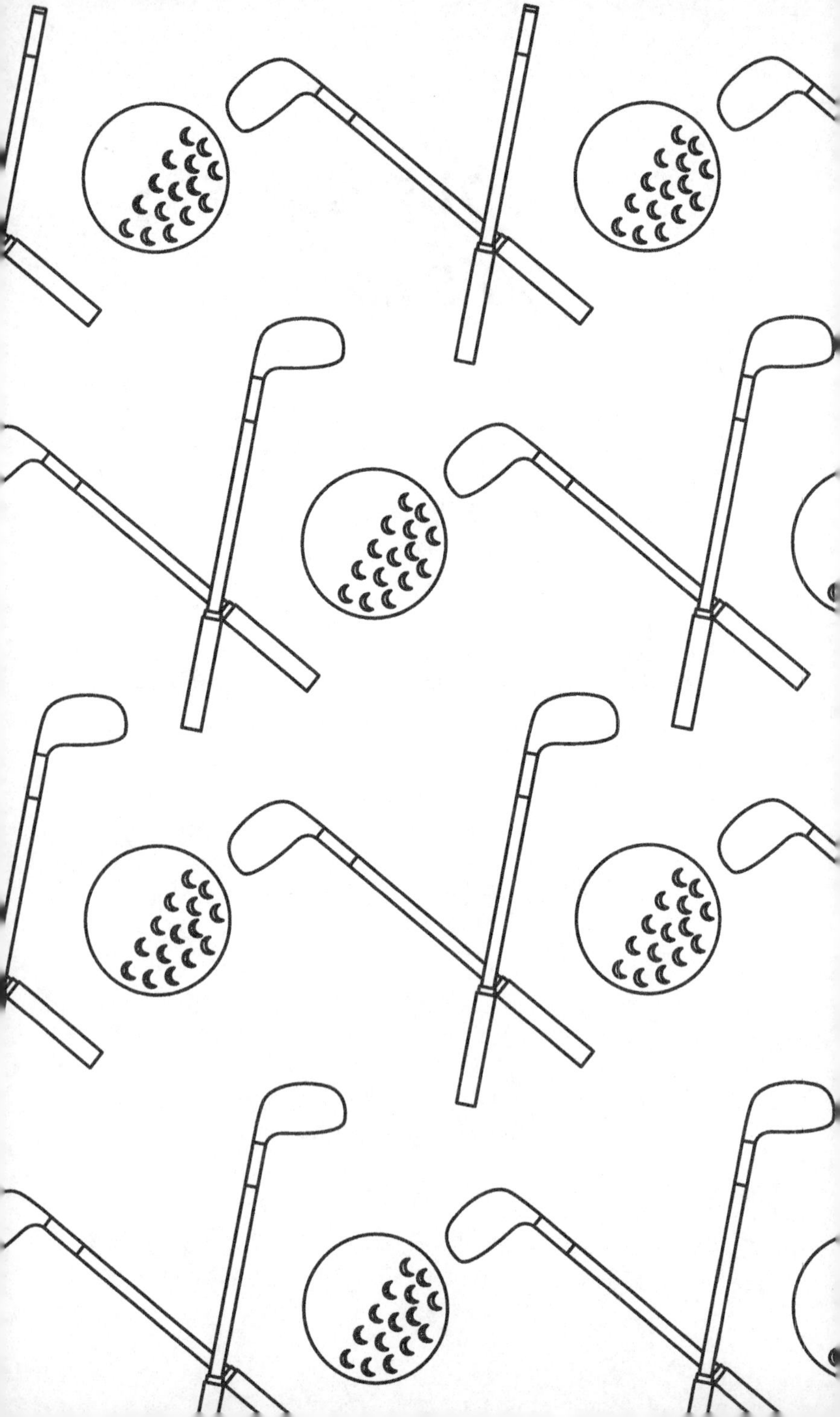

YOUR GOLF GAME IS SO BAD...

Your golf game is so bad that your caddie needs hazard pay.

Your golf game is so bad that even the bunker started feeling sorry for you.

Your golf game is so bad that your driver filed for unemployment.

Your golf game is so bad that the fairway has become an urban legend in your round.

Your golf game is so bad that even your scorecard walks away in shame.

YOUR GOLF GAME IS SO BAD...

Your golf game is so bad that you need a spotter just to tee off.

Your golf game is so bad that the ball refuses to come out of your bag.

Your golf game is so bad that you can't even putt on a straight line in a parking lot.

Your golf game is so bad that you could play a par 3 and still end up in double digits.

YOUR GOLF GAME IS SO BAD...

Your golf game is so bad that the starter asked if you were using a slingshot instead of clubs.

Your golf game is so bad that your golf shoes have never set foot on the fairway.

Your golf game is so bad that your scorecard looks like a phone number.

Your golf game is so bad that your swing looks like you're trying to chop firewood.

YOUR GOLF GAME IS SO BAD...

Your golf game is so bad that the flagstick starts swaying like a snake charmer when you approach.

Your golf game is so bad that the ball begged for mercy before you hit it.

Your golf game is so bad that even the beverage cart avoids you.

Your golf game is so bad that you spent more time in the clubhouse than on the course.

YOUR GOLF GAME IS SO BAD...

Your golf game is so bad that the driving range instructor recommended you take up tennis.

Your golf game is so bad that your caddie needs a map, not a yardage book.

Your golf game is so bad that you've turned the scorecard into an art project.

Your golf game is so bad that you couldn't hit a ball in a batting cage.

YOUR GOLF GAME IS SO BAD...

Your golf game is so bad that even your putter laughs when it's time to line up.

Your golf game is so bad that you need a compass just to get out of the rough.

Your golf game is so bad that the clubhouse got a hazard warning just for you.

Your golf game is so bad that you need to book tee times for the cart path.

YOUR GOLF GAME IS SO BAD...

Your golf game is so bad that even the squirrels leave nuts out as a peace offering.

Your golf game is so bad that the starter calls you "The Ball Butcher."

Your golf game is so bad that your swing makes Happy Gilmore look like a pro.

Your golf game is so bad that you use more tees than most people use pencils.

YOUR GOLF GAME IS SO BAD...

Your golf game is so bad that the birds have filed a noise complaint.

Your golf game is so bad that your caddie switched to an insurance policy.

Your golf game is so bad that you've got a bunker membership card.

Your golf game is so bad that even the GPS on the cart gives up halfway.

YOUR GOLF GAME IS SO BAD...

Your golf game is so bad that your driver asked for a stress leave.

Your golf game is so bad that the divots on the course formed a support group.

Your golf game is so bad that even your shadow steps away during a swing.

Your golf game is so bad that the driving range asked you not to return.

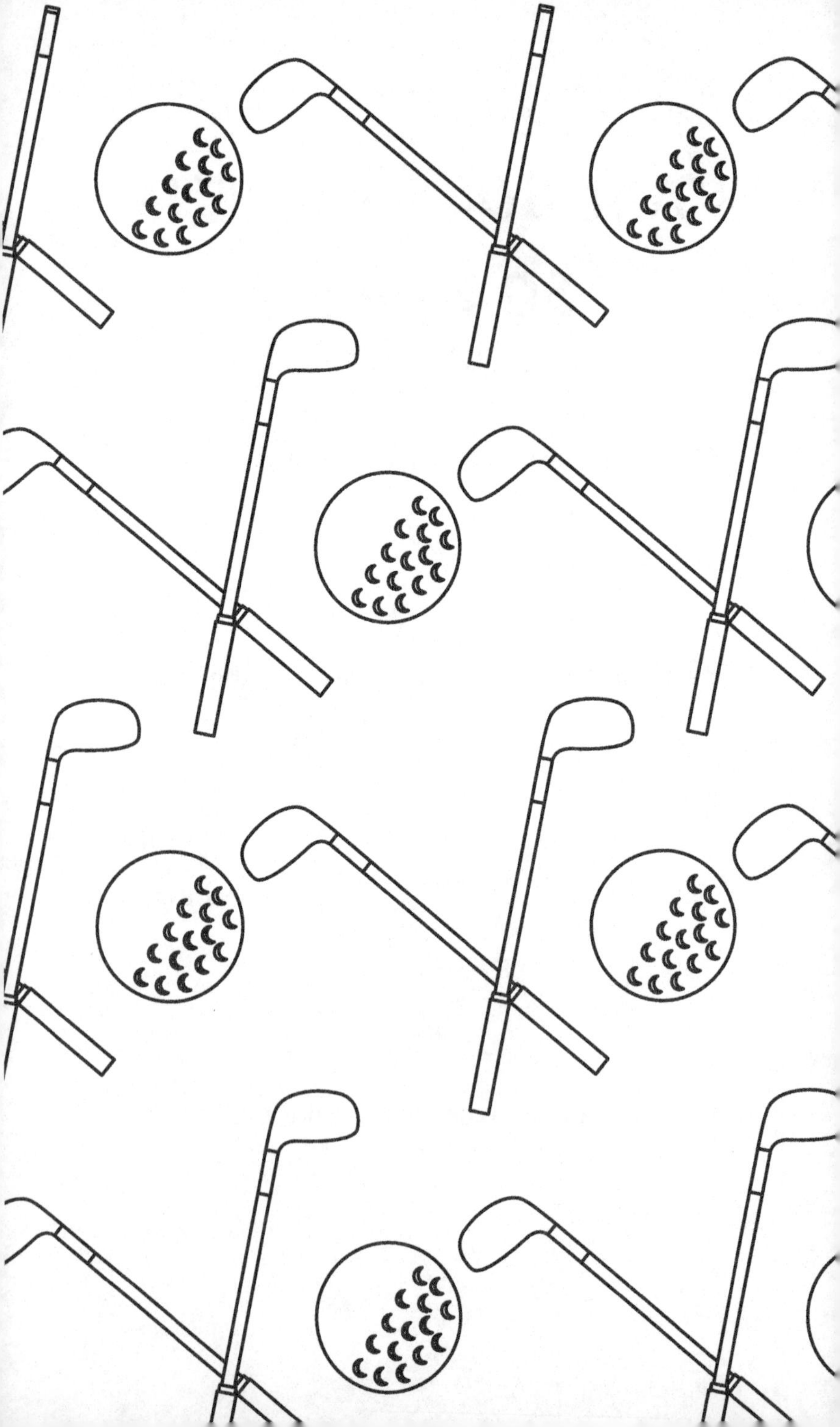

YOUR GOLF GAME IS SO BAD...

Your golf game is so bad that you've perfected the art of the double bogey.

Your golf game is so bad that the sand traps get postcards from your ball.

Your golf game is so bad that your caddie keeps a rescue flare in the bag.

Your golf game is so bad that the only "birdie" you've ever hit was by accident.

Your golf game is so bad that the scorecard needs a disclaimer.

YOUR GOLF GAME IS SO BAD...

Your golf game is so bad that you've got "frequent flyer" miles on every water hazard.

Your golf game is so bad that even the geese heckle you from the pond.

Your golf game is so bad that your putter submitted a resignation letter.

Your golf game is so bad that even the flagstick knows to dodge.

YOUR GOLF GAME IS SO BAD...

Your golf game is so bad that the ball called a taxi back to the tee.

Your golf game is so bad that your golf balls asked to unionize for protection.

Your golf game is so bad that even your rangefinder gave you a side-eye.

Your golf game is so bad that you thought "backspin" was a dance move.

YOUR GOLF GAME IS SO BAD...

Your golf game is so bad that even the golf carts pull away when they see you coming.

Your golf game is so bad that your swing was banned for cruelty to golf balls.

YYour golf game is so bad that even the caddy is taking bets against you.

Your golf game is so bad that you've mastered the art of losing balls in plain sight.

YOUR GOLF GAME IS SO BAD...

Your golf game is so bad that even your glove won't give you a hand anymore.

Your golf game is so bad that your golf bag includes a snorkel as standard equipment.

Your golf game is so bad that your swing has become a cautionary tale.

Your golf game is so bad that the water hazards have "VIP" signs for you.

YOUR GOLF GAME IS SO BAD...

Your golf game is so bad that your "hole-in-one" stories are filed under fantasy.

Your golf game is so bad that the ball finds every hazard like it's GPS-guided.

Your golf game is so bad that the squirrels send you thank-you notes for all the extra balls.

Your golf game is so bad that your ball retriever has its own ball retriever.

YOUR GOLF GAME IS SO BAD...

Your golf game is so bad that you turn every fairway into a scavenger hunt.

Your golf game is so bad that you've spent more time in the sand than a lifeguard.

Your golf game is so bad that the course has considered naming a bunker after you.

Your golf game is so bad that your scorecard is now a "Choose Your Own Adventure" book.

YOUR GOLF GAME IS SO BAD...

Your golf game is so bad that even the sprinklers don't water your divots out of respect.

Your golf game is so bad that even the scorecard told you, "It's not me; it's you."

Your golf game is so bad that you bring a hiking map to navigate the fairway.

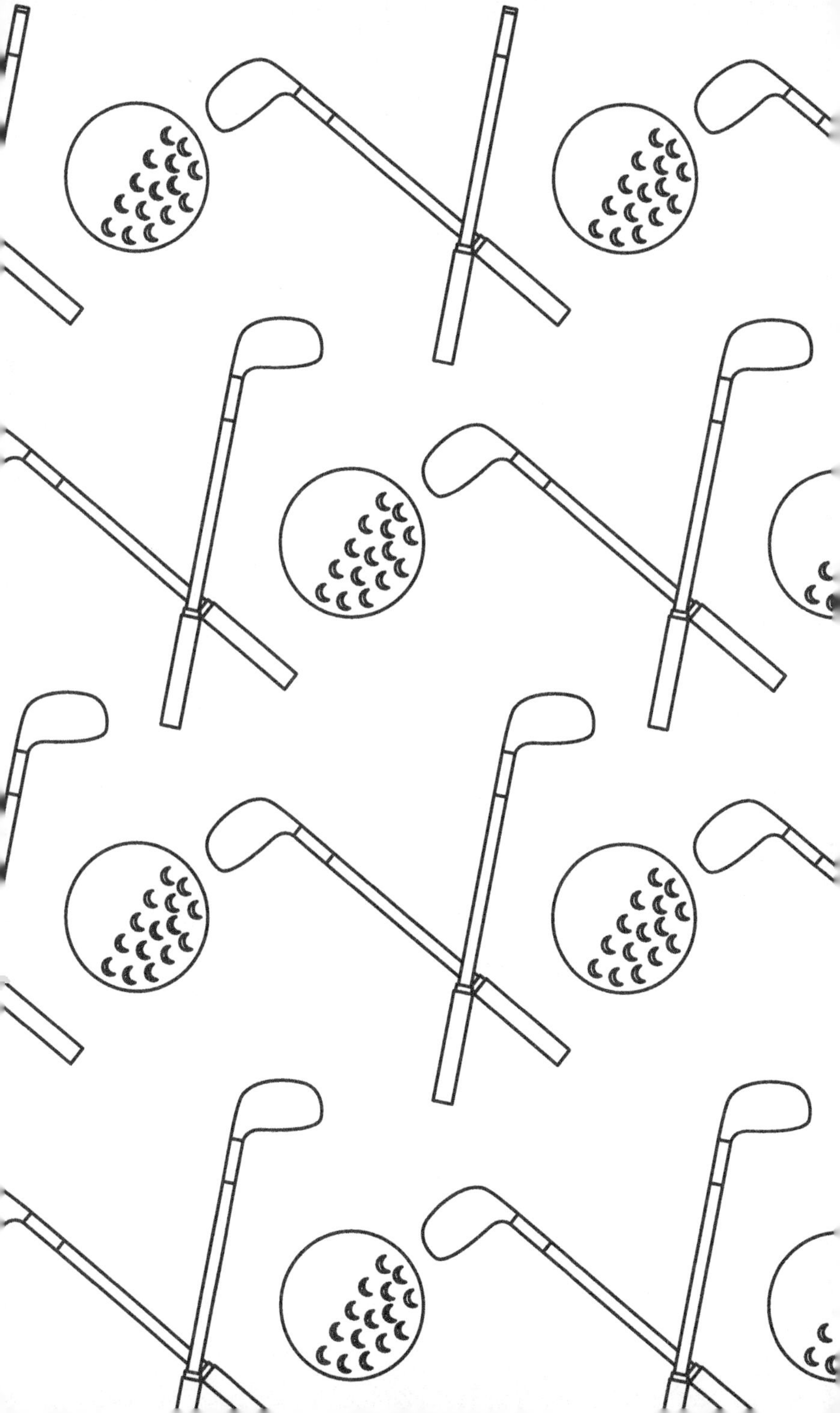

Bonus Section

THE ULTIMATE LIST OF CHEERS FOR THE 19TH HOLE

CHEERS FOR THE 19TH HOLE

To breaking par... or just breaking even!

To the longest drives and the shortest memories!

To drives that soar and putts that score!

Here's to a game that's 90% mental... and 10% forgetting last week's score!

CHEERS FOR THE 19TH HOLE

To birdies, bogeys, and beers – may we have more of the first and last!

Cheers to the 19th hole – the only one we can't miss!

May our swings be smooth and our mulligans unlimited!

Here's to fairways and greens... and forgetting what happened on the last hole!